This Book Belong To

....

L E O P A R D S
Coloring Book

Copyright © 2020 by idesig Nex studio

coco studio
1233 Pennsylvania Avenue
San Francisco, CA 94909

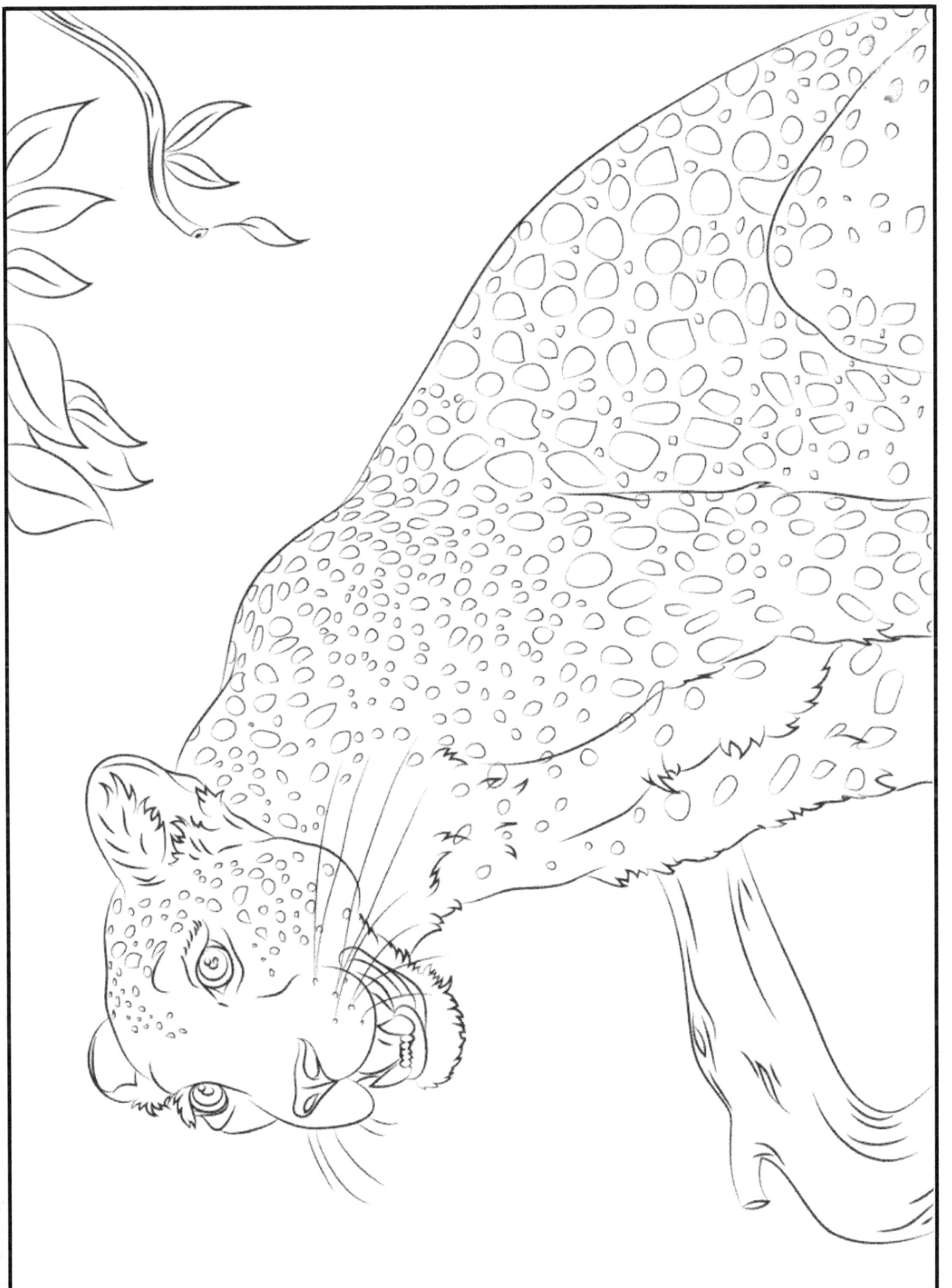

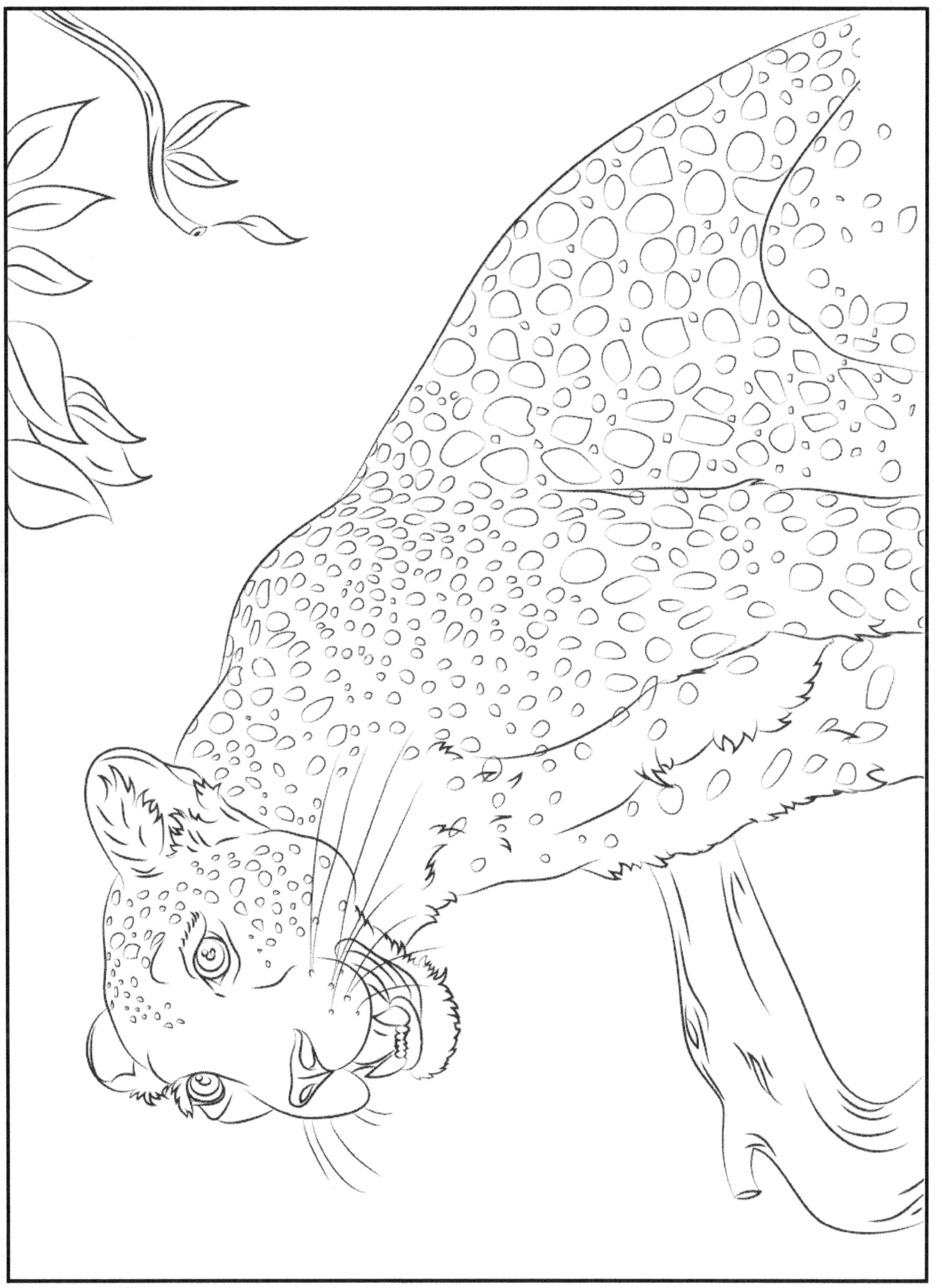

4to40

CONGRALUTIONS, YOU HAVE COMPLETED YOUR BOOK

Rating: ☆☆☆☆☆

Thank You for your trusting us